THE LAST MAN – Cycles

Brian K. Vaughan
Writer

Pia Guerra
Penciller

José Marzán, Jr.
Inker

Pamela Rambo
Colorist

Clem Robins
Letterer

J.G. Jones
Original series covers

Y: THE LAST MAN created by Brian K. Vaughan and Pia Guerra

Y: THE LAST MAN — CYCLES

DC Comics, 1700 Broadway, New York, NY 10019
A Warner Bros. Entertainment Company.
Printed in Canada. Fourth printing.
ISBN: 1-4012-0076-1
Cover illustration by J.G. Jones.
Publication design by Louis Prandi.
Logo design by Terry Marks.

THE END OF THE WORLD AS WE KNOW IT

In the summer of 2002, a plague of unknown origin destroyed every last sperm, fetus, and fully developed mammal with a Y chromosome — with the apparent exception of one young man and his pet, a male Capuchin monkey.

This "gendercide" instantaneously exterminated 48% of the global population, or approximately 2.9 billion men. 495 of the Fortune 500 CEOs are now dead, as are 99% of the world's landowners.

In the United States alone, more than 95% of all commercial pilots, truck drivers, and ship captains died... as did 92% of all violent felons. Internationally, 99% of all mechanics, electricians, and construction workers are now deceased... though 51% of the planet's *agricultural* labor force is still alive.

14 nations, including Spain and Germany, have women soldiers who have served in ground combat units. *None* of the United States' nearly 200,000 female troops have ever participated in ground combat. Australia, Norway, and Sweden are the only countries that have women serving on board submarines.

In Israel, all women between the ages of 18 and 26 have performed compulsory military service in the Israeli Defense Force for at least one year and nine months. Before the Plague, at least three Palestinian suicide bombers had been women.

Worldwide, 85% of all government representatives are now dead... as are 100% of Catholic priests, Muslim imams, and Orthodox Jewish rabbis.

Still alive, however, is Yorick Brown, the last man on Earth. The son of a United States Congresswoman, Yorick made his way to Washington, D.C. after the Plague struck to reunite with his mother, who was struggling to keep the machinery of American democracy operating. With the arrival of the new President (the former Secretary of Agriculture), Yorick found himself enlisted to track down a cloning specialist named Dr. Allison Mann and, hopefully, to aid her in whatever actions she could take to prevent the extinction of the human race. Together with Agent 355 — an extremely capable representative of one of the government's most shadowy covert agencies — Yorick and his monkey Ampersand located Dr. Mann at her lab in Boston.

Unfortunately, news as big as a living man is hard to keep a secret, both close to home and halfway around the world. An encounter with some members of a radical, man-hating group called the Daughters of the Amazon on the way to Boston demonstrated to Yorick and 355 some of the dangers they would face in traveling through post-male America, but there was no way they could have predicted the actions of an Israeli military team that's secretly tracking the Last Man as well — upon finding Dr. Mann's lab empty, they proceeded to burn it to the ground.

Now Yorick, 355, and Dr. Mann face a stark choice. Yorick is desperate to reunite with his girlfriend, last heard from in Australia, while 355 has orders to return everyone to Washington. But if they want to stick with the mission of helping Dr. Mann's research, they'll need to retrieve the backups of her data and her samples — and that means a long and dangerous trip to California.

Boston, Massachusetts
Now

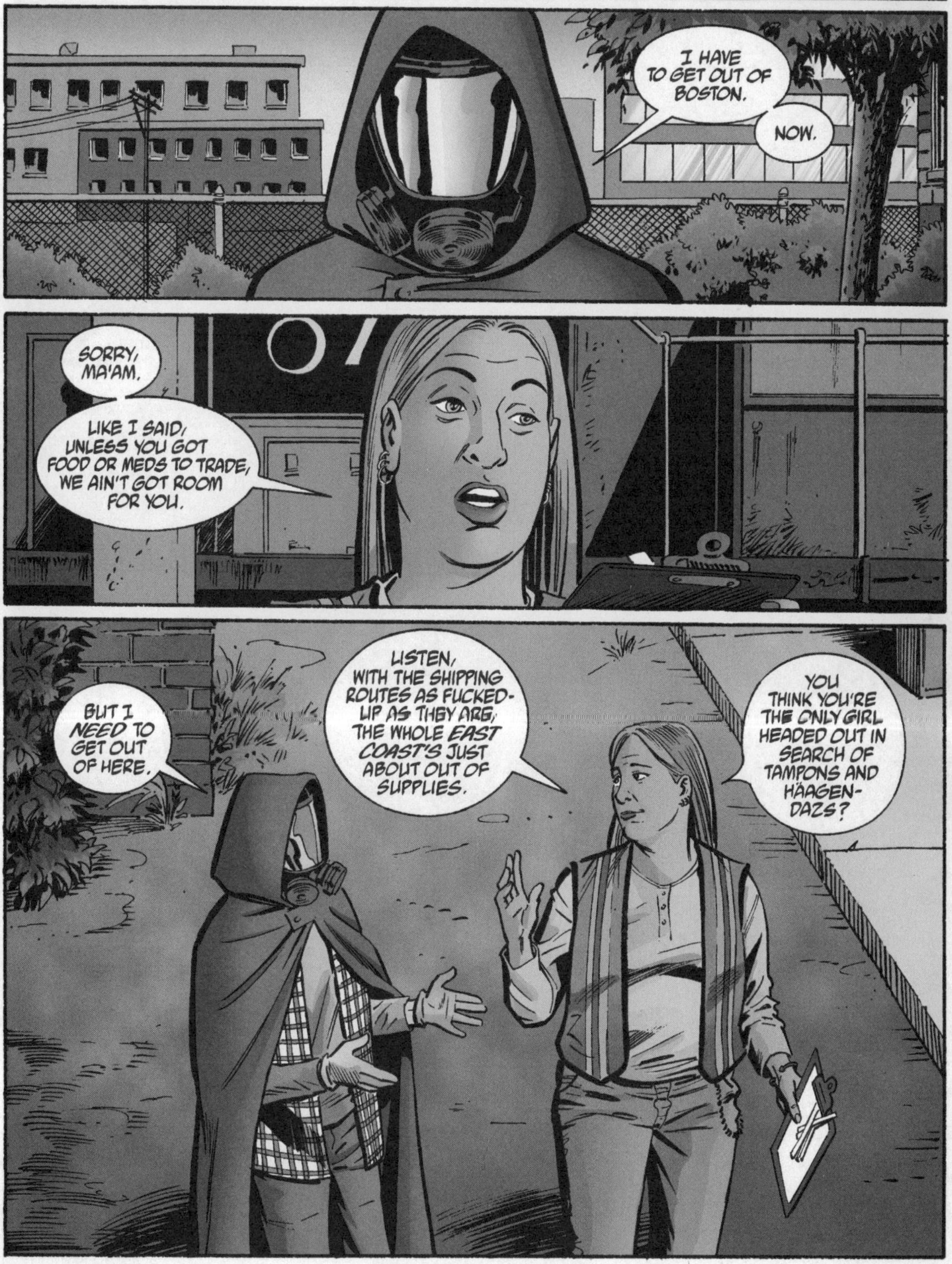

BUT I *NEED* TO GET OUT OF HERE.

LISTEN, WITH THE SHIPPING ROUTES AS FUCKED-UP AS THEY ARE, THE WHOLE *EAST COAST'S* JUST ABOUT OUT OF SUPPLIES.

YOU THINK YOU'RE THE *ONLY* GIRL HEADED OUT IN SEARCH OF TAMPONS AND HÄAGEN-DAZS?

CYCLES
CHAPTER ONE
BRIAN K. VAUGHAN PIA GUERRA
WRITER/CO-CREATORS/PENCILLER
JOSE MARZAN, JR., INKER
CLEM ROBINS, LETTERER PAMELA RAMBO, COLORIST
DIGITAL CHAMELEON, SEPARATIONS J.G. JONES, COVER ARTIST
STEVE BUNCHE, EDITOR
Y:THE LAST MAN CREATED BY
BRIAN K. VAUGHAN AND PIA GUERRA
8752
THINK AGAIN.

I MEAN, YOU KNOW HOW MANY *PLANES* WENT DOWN WHEN ALL THE MEN DIED?
WHAT DOES THAT HAVE TO DO WITH--
THERE WERE SOMETHING LIKE *FIVE THOUSAND* IN THE AIR WHEN THE PLAGUE HIT, AND THERE ARE PRACTICALLY *NO* CHICK PILOTS... SO YOU FIGURE IT OUT.

THESE OLD *DIESEL TRAINS* ARE THE ONLY WAY ANYBODY'S COVERING ANY REAL GROUND NOWADAYS.
IF YOU DON'T HAVE SOMETHING BETTER THAN THAT USELESS *GAS MASK* TO DONATE, YOU SHOULD GET IN LINE WITH EVERYBODY ELSE.
HOLD ON!

WHAT ABOUT *MOTORCYCLES?* I KNOW THE HIGHWAYS ARE STILL CONGESTED WITH ALL THE... THE DEAD GUYS IN THEIR CARS AND SHIT, BUT BIKES ARE A LITTLE MORE MANEUVERABLE THAN--
HOGS ARE TOUGHER TO SCORE THAN DOUBLE-A BATTERIES FOR YOUR *VIBRATOR*, LADY. YOU'LL *NEVER* FIND ONE.

ACTUALLY... I ALREADY DID.

MAN ALIVE.

WAIT... *WHAT* DID YOU SAY?

HUH?
OH. SORRY. OLD EXPRESSION. KINDA INAPPROPRIATE THESE DAYS, HUH?

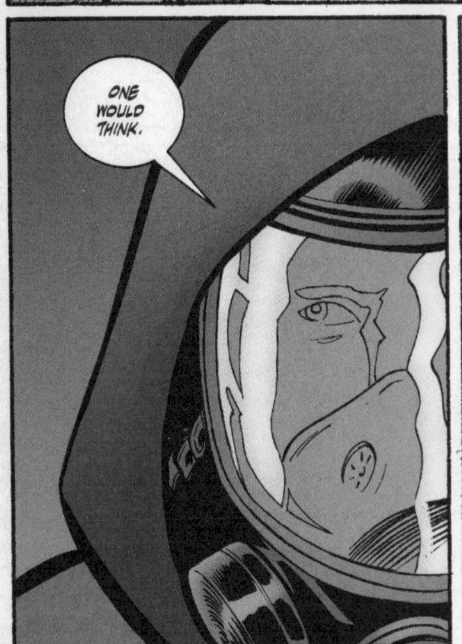
ONE WOULD THINK.

WHERE THE HELL'D YOU FIND THIS THING, ANYWAY?
MY...MY BOYFRIEND USED TO RIDE ONE JUST LIKE IT.
LONG STORY. BUT IF YOU LET ME ON BOARD, THE BIKE'S ALL YOURS. OUR LITTLE SECRET.

WELL, I...I COULDN'T GET YOU INTO PASSENGER.
CARGO, MAYBE...
DEAL.

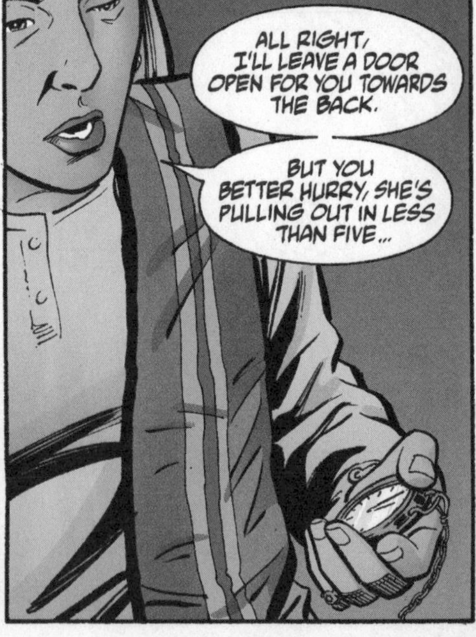
ALL RIGHT, I'LL LEAVE A DOOR OPEN FOR YOU TOWARDS THE BACK.
BUT YOU BETTER HURRY, SHE'S PULLING OUT IN LESS THAN FIVE...

355! DR. MANN!
LET'S GO!

HE ACTUALLY GOT US ON BOARD?
I TOLD YOU, DOCTOR, YORICK'S MORE RESOURCEFUL THAN HE LOOKS.
WELL, I'M JUST GLAD WE DIDN'T HAVE TO SHOOT OUR WAY INSIDE, OR WHATEVER BUTCH CASSIDY NONSENSE YOU HAD PLANNED.

I WASN'T GOING TO KILL ANY-ONE, I JUST--
CHILL, LADIES.
THERE'S NOTHING TO WORRY ABOUT. WE'VE GOT AN ENTIRE CAR TO OURSELVES. EVERY-THING IS...

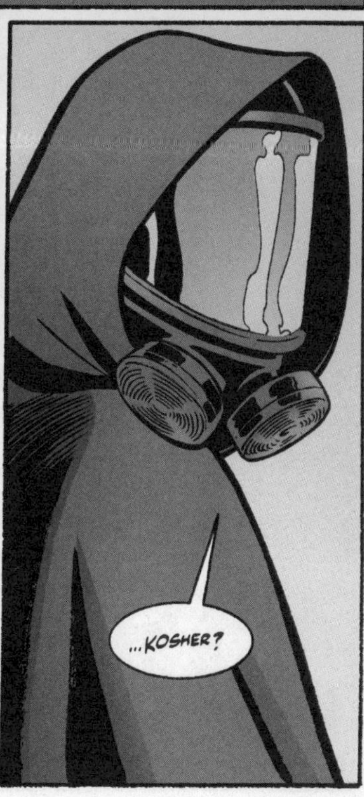
...KOSHER?

PIGS? WE HAVE TO RIDE ACROSS THE ENTIRE COUNTRY WITH PIGS?
WELL, LOOK ON THE BRIGHT SIDE, 355... AT LEAST YOU'RE NOT THE ONLY BORE ON THIS TRAIN.
GET IT? "BORE"?
ACTUALLY, THESE ARE SOWS. THE PLAGUE KILLED ALL OF THE BOARS.

8752

WHAT'S WITH THE MOSSBERG? WE HAVING BACON FOR DINNER?
AFRAID NOT. THERE ARE PEOPLE OUT THERE WHO NEED THESE ANIMALS MORE THAN WE DO.
I'M JUST BEING CAUTIOUS... IN CASE WHOEVER BURNED DOWN DR. MANN'S OLD LAB IS *FOLLOWING* US.

YOU TWO HAVE RUN INTO TROUBLE BEFORE?
OH, YOU KNOW, THE USUAL... KIDNAPPERS, AMAZONS, REPUBLICANS. NOTHING SOMEONE LIKE *YOU* WILL HAVE ANY TROUBLE HANDLING.

WHY? BECAUSE I'M *ASIAN?*
YOU THINK THAT AUTOMATICALLY MAKES ME SOME KIND OF... OF *MARTIAL ARTS* MASTER? BECAUSE I DON'T KNOW THE FIRST THING ABOUT KARATE OR KUNG FU OR--
WHOA, RELAX! I JUST MEANT YOU LOOKED PRETTY *RIPPED,* THAT'S ALL.

OH.
THANK YOU.
I...USED TO BE INTO PILATES.

BUT SINCE YOU BRING IT UP, WHAT NATIONALITY *ARE* YOU?
:SIGH:
MY *NATIONALITY* IS AMERICAN. MY *ETHNICITY* IS CHINESE AND JAPANESE.

REALLY? I DIDN'T THINK RELATIONS WERE PARTICULARLY STRONG BETWEEN THOSE GROUPS.
WELL, MY MOTHER AND FATHER CERTAINLY DIDN'T GET ALONG.
SHE WAS A SURGEON, HE WAS A RESEARCH SCIENTIST. THEY FELL IN LOVE AT A CONFERENCE IN TAIWAN, MOVED TO THE STATES... AND SPENT THE REST OF THEIR LIVES *SCREAMING* AT EACH OTHER.

SO IS YOUR LAST NAME CHINESE OR JAPANESE?
NEITHER. I CHANGED IT MY FIRST YEAR AT BERKELEY.
WHY "MANN"?

AFTER MANN'S CHINESE THEATER IN LOS ANGELES. I WANTED SOMETHING KITSCH-Y AND FAUX-ASIAN TO INSULT MY FATHER.
JESUS. YOU MUST HAVE REALLY HATED THE GUY.

I STILL DO.
HIS DEATH IS THE ONE GOOD THING TO COME OUT OF THIS HOLOCAUST.

YIKES.
UH...
HOW'D YOU END UP IN BOSTON?

I GOT A JOB TEACHING BIOTECH AT HARVARD. I WAS TENURED THERE AFTER--
TENURED? CHRIST, HOW OLD ARE YOU?

GOOD LORD, YORICK. DO YOU HAVE ANY TACT?
IT'S ALL RIGHT. I'M THIRTY-ONE, ANCIENT COMPARED TO YOU TWO.
FUCK! MY DAD DIDN'T BECOME A FULL PROFESSOR UNTIL HE WAS FORTY.

HE WAS AT HARVARD?
NAH, HE TAUGHT SHAKESPEARE AT THIS LITTLE ALL-WOMEN'S COLLEGE.
THE CLOSEST DAD EVER GOT TO THE BIG H WAS VISITING MY SISTER, HERO. SHE WORKED AROUND CAMBRIDGE.

HAVE YOU SEEN YOUR SISTER SINCE THE PLAGUE?
UH-UH, AGENT 355 AND I NEVER DID FIND HER. BUT KNOW-ING HERO, SHE'S PROBABLY VOLUNTEER-ING SOMEWHERE, DOING HER FLO NIGHTINGALE THING...

Boston's Fenway Park
Now

LOOK AT ME LIKE THAT AGAIN... AND I'LL KNEEL ON YOUR THROAT UNTIL YOU FUCKING *DIE*.

HERO!

GET OVER HERE! WHAT THE HELL IS WRONG WITH YOU? YOU'VE BEEN LASHING OUT LIKE THIS EVER SINCE WE LEFT CONNECTICUT.
WE'RE ALL IRRITATED THAT WE HAVEN'T CAUGHT THIS MALE WHO'S SUPPOSEDLY OUT THERE, BUT THAT'S NO EXCUSE FOR --
IT'S NOT THAT, VICTORIA, IT'S... NOTHING.

AH.
YOU'RE STILL UPSET ABOUT WHAT HAPPENED TO THAT GIRL.
SOMETHING DIDN'T "HAPPEN." I... I MURDERED HER.

YOU ENDED HER SUFFERING, HERO. SHE WAS STILL CLINGING TO THE OLD WORLD. YOU SET HER FREE.
IT'S UNFORTUNATE THAT WE HAD TO USE VIOLENCE, BUT AS LONG AS ONE MAN IS STILL ALIVE ON THIS PLANET, WE HAVE NO CHOICE BUT TO PLAY BY THEIR RULES.
I'M SO HUNGRY. ALL I THINK ABOUT IS PASTA AND... AND SOME-TIMES, I... I WANT TO CUT MY FINGERS OFF. WHY DO I WANT THAT? I--

HERO, MOTHER EARTH SENT YOU TO ME FOR A REASON. YOUR KNOWLEDGE OF THIS CITY HAS BEEN INVALU-ABLE, AND YOU'RE AN INSPIRATION TO EVERY DAUGHTER OF THE AMAZON.
HERE, I WANT YOU TO HAVE SOME-THING...

THIS IS A SPECIAL SUPPLEMENT TO YOUR RATIONS. OF COURSE, I'D APPRECIATE IT IF YOU DIDN'T TELL OUR SISTERS ABOUT IT.
FOR ...FOR ME?
STRAWBERRY

I... I LOVE YOU, VICTORIA.
I LOVE YOU SO MUCH...

YOU KNOW, I'VE EATEN SO MANY CANNED PEACHES OVER THE LAST FEW MONTHS, I ACTUALLY SHAT A *COBBLER* LAST NIGHT.
GOD, YOU MAKE ME WANT TO PUKE.
OH, THAT'S PROBABLY JUST THE SMELL OF OUR FESTERING LIVE-STOCK CAR.

HOW DO THESE... *ACCOMMODATIONS* COMPARE TO OTHER PLACES YOU TWO HAVE STAYED?
PRETTY FAVOR-ABLY, BELIEVE IT OR NOT. YORICK AND I HAVE BEEN TRYING TO KEEP A LOW PROFILE, SO WE USUALLY STICK TO EMPTY CAMPSITES.
ACTUALLY, BEFORE I LEFT NEW YORK FOR D.C., I SPENT ONE NIGHT IN THE PRESIDENTIAL SUITE OF THE FOUR SEASONS.

YOU DID? *WHY?*
BECAUSE I COULD?
IT WAS MOSTLY SAD THOUGH. THE WHOLE JOINT WAS PACKED WITH HOMELESS WOMEN, AND THEY DIDN'T EXACTLY SEEM... *DISTRAUGHT* ABOUT THE TURN OF EVENTS, YOU KNOW?

"AND THE MEEK SHALL INHERIT THE EARTH," AND ALL THAT...
MADE ME WONDER IF THIS WHOLE THING HAPPENED FOR A REASON.

WHO ARE YOU CALLING MEEK, ASSHOLE?
YOU KNOW WHAT I MEAN.
HEY, YOU HAVE ANY IDEA WHERE WE ARE NOW?

AFTER SEVEN HOURS? PENNSYLVANIA, PROBABLY. MAYBE OHIO.
SERIOUSLY? ALL THESE TOWNS LOOK THE SAME IN THE DARK. IS IT THAT HARD FOR YOU LADIES TO TURN SOME LIGHTS ON?

ELECTRICITY DOESN'T COME THROUGH THE SOCKETS MAGICALLY, YORICK. IT TAKES A LOT OF MANPOWER... HUMAN-POWER TO OPERATE ALL OF THE PLANTS AND SUB-STATIONS.
AND THE CULPER RING IS ALREADY WORKING TO GET THEM RUNNING AGAIN.
THERE ARE MORE OF YOU SECRET AGENT TYPES OUT THERE?

OF COURSE. AND NOT ALL OF US ARE BUSY BABYSITTING AMATEUR MAGICIANS.
ACTUALLY, I PREFER ILLUSIONIST. OR ESCAPE ARTIST, OR--
AS A MATTER OF FACT, WHEN I'M DONE WITH YOU, I STILL HAVE TO FINISH THE MISSION I STARTED BEFORE THE PLAGUE.

OH, YEAH?
DOES IT HAVE SOME-THING TO DO WITH THIS?

WHERE THE HELL DID YOU GET THAT?
OH, UH... AMPERSAND WAS PLAYING WITH IT EARLIER. HE MUST HAVE PULLED IT OUT OF YOUR BAG WHEN HE WAS SCROUNGING FOR SNACKS.
IF IT'S VALUABLE, YOU SHOULD REALLY BE MORE--

THANK YOU.
WHAT IS IT, ANYWAY?
LOOKS LIKE THAT OLD MEDALLION SHARPTON USED TO WEAR.

IT'S CALLED THE AMULET OF HELENE.
IT'S... CLASSIFIED.

IF I HAD A NICKEL FOR EVERY TIME YOU USED THAT WORD, I'D HAVE--
YOU WOULDN'T HAVE SHIT, BITCH.

'CAUSE EVERYTHING YOU GOT BELONGS TO US.

AMAZONS?

HELL, NO. THE FTRA WAS AROUND LONG BEFORE THOSE SLITS.
AND IF YOU WANNA RIDE OUR RAILS, YOU GOTTA PAY A TOLL FOR--

HEY.
IS THAT A DUDE?

YOU GET NATTY GANN, I'LL GO FOR BOXCAR BERTHA.
JUST STAY BACK, YORICK.

I'LL TAKE CARE OF THIS.

NO GUNS!

NIGGER'S GOT A PIECE!
NOT FOR LONG.

NO!

GET THE FUCK...

...OFFA ME!

YORICK!

UHN!

FUH--

I--I'M SO SORRY. I JUST--
SAVE IT.
WE'RE GOING AFTER HIM.
I CAN'T JUMP OUT OF A MOVING TRAIN!
YOU CAN AND YOU WILL. NOW LET'S GO! THE LONGER WE ARGUE, THE FURTHER AWAY WE GET FROM YORICK!
GO WITHOUT ME! I CAN MAKE IT TO SAN FRANCISCO ON MY OWN! YOU TWO CAN MEET ME AFTER--
YOU'RE MY RESPONSIBILITY NOW, DOCTOR. BESIDES, HOW LONG DO YOU THINK YOU'LL LAST WITH TWO PSYCHOTIC HOBOS IN YOUR CAR?
YOU CAN JUST THROW THEM OUT THE DOOR, 355!
GOOD IDEA.
125
AHHHHHHHH!

VICTORIA, I THINK WE MAY HAVE SOMETHING.
WHAT IS IT?
WE FOUND THIS WOMAN DOWNTOWN. SAYS SHE HAS INFORMATION ABOUT *MEN*.

PLEASE...YOU MUST BE HELPING ME. MY NAME IS *NATALYA*. YOU MUST HELP ME TO GET TO THE MEN. I KNOW WHERE TO...*ehh*, WHERE THEY ARE *LOCATED*.
AS IN MORE THAN *ONE*? WHAT DO YOU KNOW, SISTER?
STILL ALIVE? WHERE?

KOSMICHESKAYA. HOW DO YOU SAY...
SPACE.

I SEE.
TELL ME, NATALYA, THESE "MEN"...THEY WOULDN'T HAPPEN TO BE LITTLE? AND GREEN? AND FROM THE PLANET MARS, NOW WOULD THEY?

THIS WOMAN IS DELIRIOUS, BECCA. YOU'VE WASTED OUR TIME. GIVE HER SOME OF YOUR RATIONS AND SEND HER ON HER WAY.
NO! PLEASE!

I TRAVEL ALL THE WAY FROM MOSCOW! YOU MUST HELP ME GET TO THE KANSAS! THE SOYUZ! THE SOYUZ IS COMING TO THE KANSAS! POZHALUJSTA!
ANYTHING FROM YOUR TEAM, JOANNE?
NOTHING CONCRETE...THOUGH WE DID TALK WITH A WOMAN WHO SAID SHE SAW SOME-ONE ON A MOTORCYCLE HEADED FOR THE RAIL YARD.

WAS THE RIDER WEARING A GAS MASK?
SHE WASN'T POSITIVE, BUT...
I'M SURE THIS WAS JUST THE HUNGER TALKING, BUT SHE SWORE THAT WHO-EVER WAS ON THE BIKE WAS CARRYING A...A MONKEY.
A MON--?

NO.
IT...IT COULDN'T BE.

Marrisville, Ohio
Nine Hours Later

THANK YOU, JESUS.

CROSSING

Marrisville, Ohio
Now

GOD.
THAT... THAT WAS GREAT.

THEY'RE NOT EVEN SCRATCHED.
I JUMPED OUT OF A GODDAMN MOVING TRAIN AND MY GLASSES AREN'T EVEN SCRATCHED.

HOW ABOUT YOU, 355?

YOU OKAY?
CYCLES
CHAPTER TWO
BRIAN K. VAUGHAN PIA GUERRA
WRITER / CO-CREATORS / PENCILLER
JOSE MARZAN, JR., INKER
CLEM ROBINS, LETTERER PAMELA RAMBO, COLORIST
ZYLONOL, SEPARATIONS J.G. JONES, COVER ARTIST
STEVE BUNCHE, EDITOR
Y: THE LAST MAN CREATED BY BRIAN K. VAUGHAN AND PIA GUERRA

CAN YOU HEAR ME?
DON'T BE AFRAID.
I'M NOT GOING TO HURT YOU.
BETH...?
WHO'S BETH?
AHH!

WHAT THE FUCK IS HAPPENING?
TAKE IT EASY.

WHO THE FUCK ARE YOU?
MY NAME'S SONIA. I...I FOUND YOU. WITH YOUR PET. YOU WERE UNCONSCIOUS OUT BY OUR WELL.
WHERE THE FUCK AM I?

MARRISVILLE. IN OHIO?
WHERE DID YOU COME FROM, YORICK? I THOUGHT ALL THE MEN WERE--
WAIT, HOW THE HELL DO YOU KNOW MY NAME?

OH, IT WAS ON YOUR MEMBERSHIP CARD FOR THE, um..."INTERNATIONAL BROTHERHOOD OF MAGICIANS."

ARE YOU REALLY A MAGICIAN? LIKE DAVID BLAINE?
IS THAT HOW YOU SURVIVED? YOU...YOU ESCAPED DEATH?
NO, I AM NOTHING LIKE DAVID BLAINE, THANK YOU VERY MUCH. I'M AN ESCAPE ARTIST.

THAT'S CUTE.
BUT LISTEN, I REALLY HAVE TO GET OUT OF HERE.
ACTUALLY... YOU SHOULD PROBABLY STAY PUT.

AND WHY'S THAT?

um...

JESUS!
WHAT DID YOU DO WITH MY *PANTS*?

I PUT 'EM IN THE WASH. THEY WERE KINDA... *DIRTY*, YORICK.
I THINK YOU HAD, LIKE, AN *ACCIDENT* IN THEM.

ACCIDENT?
CHRIST, THAT'S RIGHT...SOME DERANGED HOBO WAS PLAYING THROW MAMA FROM THE TRAIN WITH ME.
THAT'S HOW YOU ENDED UP HERE?

UNLESS I DREAMT IT. WHY, YOU THINK I JUST DROPPED OUT OF THE SKY?
I DIDN'T KNOW WHAT TO THINK. I FIGURED YOU MIGHT BE LIKE NEWTON OR SOMETHING, YOU KNOW?
WHO?

GUY FROM THE MAN WHO FELL TO EARTH?
SERIOUSLY? I DIDN'T THINK PRETTY GIRLS WERE INTO THAT KIND OF STUFF. YOU A FAN OF THE BOOK OR THE MOVIE?
BOTH ACTUALLY. BUT...MOSTLY BOWIE, TO BE HONEST.

WELL, BULLY FOR YOU.
YEAH, CHILLY FOR ME.

FAME?

WOW, I...I NEVER MET ANYONE WHO KNEW THE CORRECT LYRICS.
NOT EVEN YOUR WIFE?

MY *WHAT?*
YOUR RING.
THE INSCRIPTION SAYS, "TO MY BEAUTIFUL *WIFE*."

OH. YEAH. THAT'S FOR BETH. MY...MY *GIRL-FRIEND*. WE'RE NOT REALLY ENGAGED YET.
TECHNICALLY.

"TECHNICALLY"?
IT'S COMPLICATED. SEE, SHE'S IN AUSTRALIA RIGHT NOW, BUT I'M GONNA FIND HER RIGHT AFTER I HELP MY--

OH, FUCK.
WHAT IS IT?
MY *FRIENDS*. THEY...THEY WERE RIDING WITH ME WHEN I GOT JUMPED. I DON'T KNOW WHAT HAPPENED TO THEM.

DON'T WORRY, YORICK. I... I'M SURE THEY'RE *FINE*.

NNN...

IT'S DR. MANN. DO YOU KNOW YOUR NAME?
WHO...?
DO YOU KNOW WHAT DAY IT IS?

YEAH. IT'S... CLASSIFIED.
GOOD GIRL.

YOU SUFFERED SOME PRETTY SEVERE HEAD TRAUMA, AGENT 355. I WAS ABLE TO STOP THE BLEEDING, BUT I NEED TO GET YOU TO A MEDICAL FACIL--
NO.

USE THIS...

ABSOLUTELY NOT!
IT'S PROBABLY JUST A CONCUSSION, 355. I'M NOT GOING TO... TO PUT YOU OUT OF YOUR MISERY!

NO, USE THIS TO DEFEND YOURSELF... IN CASE THOSE WOMEN WHO ATTACKED US COME BACK.
OH.
WELL, THANK YOU, BUT GUNS AREN'T... AREN'T REALLY MY THING.

YOU'LL NEED IT. YOU'RE GOING TO HAVE TO LEAVE ME HERE, DOCTOR. I DON'T THINK I CAN WALK ON MY OWN... AND YOU CAN'T CARRY ME BY YOURSELF.
OF COURSE I CAN!

BUT YOU SHOULDN'T. YOU MIGHT... MAKE THINGS WORSE. YOU CAN COME BACK WITH HELP... LATER. RIGHT NOW, YOU HAVE MORE IMPORTANT THINGS TO DO.
LIKE WHAT?
LIKE FINDING YORICK...

...BEFORE SOMEONE ELSE DOES.

Boston, Massachusetts
Now

HERO, END THIS!
I HAVE HER!

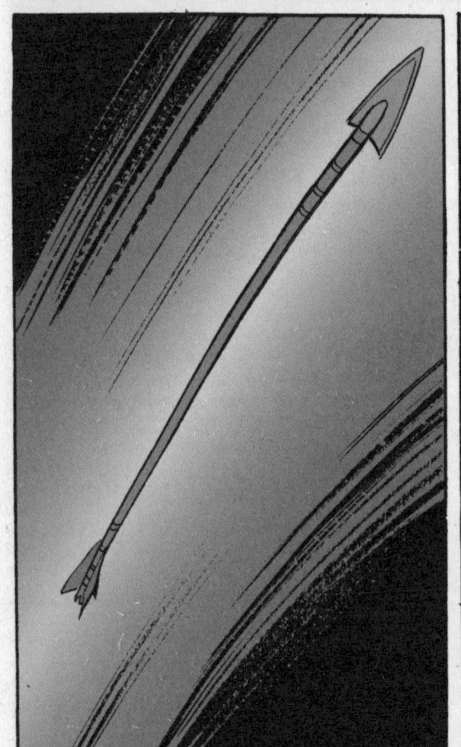

AHN!
SHUNK

ENF!

BRILLIANT SHOT, LOVE!
I WAS AIMING FOR HER TIRE...

GODDAMN.

DID YOU HONESTLY THINK YOU COULD OUTRUN US? DO YOU HAVE ANY IDEA WHO WE *ARE?*
YOU'RE THOSE, *ehn*... AMAZON-DOT-COM CHICKS.

THAT'S *DAUGHTERS* OF THE AMAZON. MY NAME IS VICTORIA, AND YOUR BIKE BELONGS TO *ME*. HOW DID IT COME TO BE IN THE POSSESSION OF A *TRAIN CONDUCTOR?*
I...I GOT IT FROM SOME GIRL IN A GAS MASK, ALL RIGHT? SHE TRADED IT FOR PASSAGE TO *CALIFORNIA*. NOW HELP ME... *PLEASE*.

ASK HER IF THE PERSON HAD A *MONKEY* WITH THEM, VICTORIA.
WILL YOU FORGET ABOUT THIS *PRIMATE*, HERO? THAT WAS OBVIOUSLY BAD INFORMATION. WE'RE LOOKING FOR A DISGUISED *MALE*, NOT A FUCKING *ORGAN GRINDER*.
LISTEN UP! IT SOUNDS AS IF WE MAY HAVE FOUND THE LAST OF THE SLAVE DRIVERS, BUT I HAVE NO INTENTION OF TRAVELING ACROSS THE ENTIRE COUNTRY ONLY TO DISCOVER THAT WE WERE GIVEN A *FALSE LEAD*.
FAN OUT AND INTERROGATE EVERY LAST DERELICT IN THE TENTS AROUND THESE TRACKS. MAKE SURE THAT SOMEONE *ELSE* SAW A GAS-MASK-CLAD FIGURE BOARD A WESTBOUND TRAIN.

AND REMEMBER, NO PRICE IS TOO GREAT FOR YOUR OPPONENT'S KING!

SO, uh...
HOW MUCH
DO I OWE YOU
FOR THE CLEAN
UNDERPANTS?

ON THE
HOUSE.
GOOD, BECAUSE THE ONLY
THING I'VE GOT TO TRADE IS
AMPERSAND...AND HE'D BE
ABOUT AS USEFUL TO YOU
AS END-STAGE
SYPHILIS.
RRRRRR

AW, I LOVE YOUR
MONKEY! HE'S
SWEET!
YEAH, WELL, SO'S THE SMELL
OF BURNING FLESH. DOESN'T
MEAN IT'S GOOD.

ANYWAY, THANKS FOR EVERY-
THING, SONIA. I REALLY APPRECIATE
THE...YOU KNOW, KINDNESS OF
STRANGERS AND ALL THAT.
YOU'RE
LEAVING? BUT...
BUT YOU HAVEN'T
EVEN MET EVERY-
ONE!

SONIA,
THIS WAS FUN--
IN A PERVERTED BACK
TO THE FUTURE KINDA
WAY--BUT I HAVE A
JOB TO DO.
BESIDES, I
SHOULD REALLY
BOOK BEFORE ANY-
ONE FINDS OUT
I'M HERE.
YORICK,
THIS IS A TOWN
OF SIXTY-SEVEN
GOSSIPING
WOMEN...

DID YOU REALLY THINK I COULD KEEP SOMETHING LIKE YOU A *SECRET?*

AH, CRAP.

MARRISVILLE, THIS IS YORICK.
YORICK, THIS IS MARRISVILLE.
PLEASURE.

THE LIGHTS. THEY'RE... THEY'RE NOT GAS LAMPS.
SO?

SO, I HAVEN'T SEEN ELECTRICITY IN WEEKS.
REALLY? GETTING OUR GRID CONTROL STATION BACK ONLINE WAS ACTUALLY PRETTY SIMPLE. SETTING UP THE HYDROPONIC GREENHOUSE WAS PROBABLY MORE DIFFICULT.

YOU HAVE FOOD? FRESH FOOD?
'COURSE. WE EVEN VOTED TO SLAUGHTER ONE OF THE COWS FOR YOU TONIGHT.
AND DON'T FEEL GUILTY. LYDIA WANTS US TO GET RID OF 'EM ANYWAY, BEFORE THEY CATCH SOME OF THE DISEASES THAT ARE STARTING TO GO AROUND.

LYDIA?
AHEM.

HARD TO BELIEVE THAT HELPLESS LITTLE WOMEN CAN GET BY WITHOUT YOUR KIND, eh?

OH, I...I DIDN'T MEAN ANY DISRESPECT, MA'AM. IT'S JUST, SOME OF THE CITIES I'VE BEEN TO LOOK LIKE THE THIRD ACT OF A GODZILLA FLICK, BUT THIS PLACE STILL SEEMS LIKE MAYBERRY.
THAT'S 'CAUSE WE'VE ALL HAD PLENTY OF EXPERIENCE MAKING DO WITHOUT ANY MEN AROUND.
LYDIA...

BACK IN '42, THE ONLY FELLAS LEFT IN THIS COUNTRY WERE THE GODDAMN 4F-ERS, TRYIN' TO GET INTO OUR OVERALLS. GIRLS WEREN'T PART OF THE WORKFORCE... WE WERE THE WORKFORCE.
I WAS FIFTEEN WHEN I STARTED BUCKING RIVETS AT LOCKHEED FOR WAR STAMPS. AT SIXTEEN, I GOT A JOB WELDING 50mm SHELL CASINGS. THERE WAS NOTHING I COULDN'T DO.

HELL, IF NONE OF OUR BOYS HAD COME HOME ALIVE, WE COULDA RUN THIS PLACE JUST FINE ON OUR OWN... BETTER, EVEN.
WAIT, YOU SAID YOU ALL HAD EXPERIENCE LIVING WITHOUT MEN. HOW'S THAT?
I MEAN, MOST OF THESE WOMEN ARE A LITTLE TOO YOUNG TO HAVE BEEN DOING THE ROSIE THE RIVETER THING WITH YOU... RIGHT?

WELL, uh, MAYBE LYDIA CAN EXPLAIN HERSELF WHILE WE FIX YOU SOME SUPPER.
I'M SORRY, SONIA, BUT I REALLY HAVE TO FIND MY--
YORICK!

DR. MANN!

IT'S COOL, LADIES. SHE'S WITH ME.
DOC, HOW DID YOU--
YORICK, IT'S --IT'S 355.

IN WHAT TIME ZONE? IT'S ALMOST 7:30 NOW.
NO, 355 IS ONE OF MY *FRIENDS*.
SHE'S A... SHE WORKS FOR THE *GOVERNMENT*.

AND SHE'S HURT. *BADLY*. I NEED A HAND TRANSPORTING HER BACK HERE. *PLEASE*.
WELL, WE... WE BUILT A MAKESHIFT STRETCHER TO CARRY *YOU*, YORICK.
SHOW US WHERE!

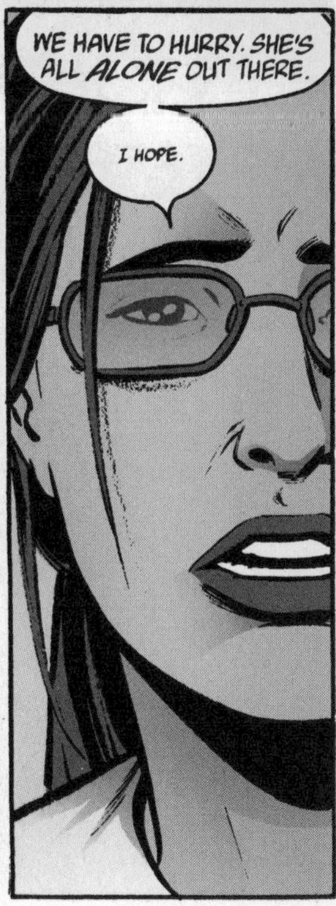
WE HAVE TO HURRY. SHE'S ALL *ALONE* OUT THERE.
I HOPE.

WELL, WELL, WELL, WHAT DO WE HAVE *HERE?*

WHAT THE FUCK *YOU* WANT, BITCH?

YOU TWO HAVE BEEN SPREADING RUMORS AROUND CAMP. TELLING PEOPLE YOU SAW A *MAN*.
EXPLAIN.
OR *WHAT?* WE'VE RUN INTO YOU AMAZONS BEFORE. YOU DYKES CAN'T WORK A BOW FOR *SHIT*.

YOU'RE ...YOU'RE RIGHT.

SO WHY DON'T YOU GO BACK TO YOUR LITTLE RUG MUNCHERS AND LEAVE US THE FUCK--

SHINK

AHHHHH!
JESUS FUCKING CHRIST!

MY FUCKING HAND!

BANG.

EASY...
PRECISELY. IT IS SO EASY TO KILL SOMEONE.
EASIER THAN DOING LAUNDRY. IT...IT EVEN SMELLS LIKE LAUNDRY. I'VE DONE IT. HAVE YOU DONE IT? KILLING, I MEAN, NOT LAUNDRY. HEH.

JESUS, SHE'S FUCKING NUTS.
SHUT IT, WINONA.

LISTEN, WE...WE DID HAVE A SIGHTING, OKAY? WHEN WE WAS COLLECTING TOLLS ON THE TWILIGHT LINER. DUDE HAD A FUCKING BABY APE WITH HIM.
WE TRIED TO NAB THE GUY, BUT ME AND MY FRIEND GOT ROLLED BY ONE OF THE CHICKS HE WAS WITH, SO WE CAUGHT US AN EASTBOUND BACK HERE AND--
THIS MAN. DID YOU CATCH HIS NAME?

YEAH, uh... RICK SOME-THING.
YORICK?!
GUESS SO. WHY, YOU...YOU KNOW HIM?

SINCE THE DAY HE WAS BORN.

HE'S TROUBLE.

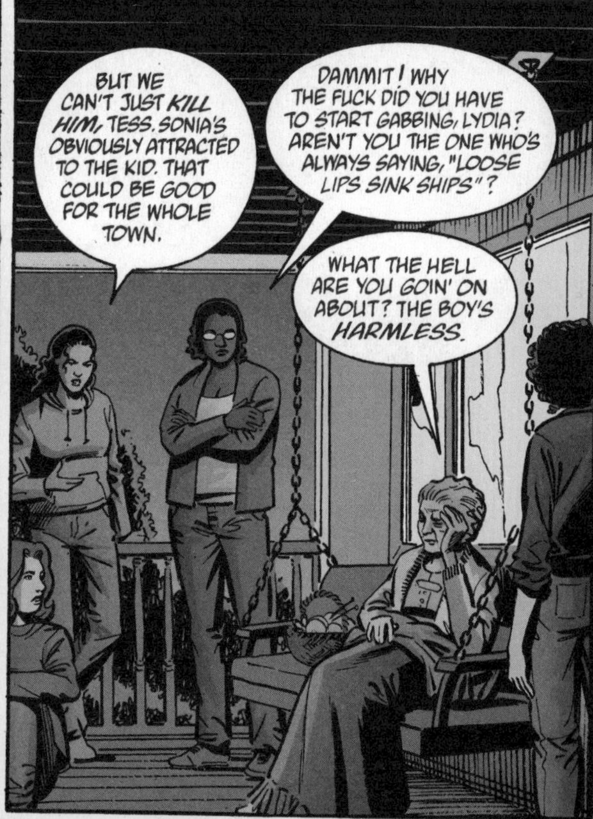
BUT WE CAN'T JUST KILL HIM, TESS. SONIA'S OBVIOUSLY ATTRACTED TO THE KID. THAT COULD BE GOOD FOR THE WHOLE TOWN.
DAMMIT! WHY THE FUCK DID YOU HAVE TO START GABBING, LYDIA? AREN'T YOU THE ONE WHO'S ALWAYS SAYING, "LOOSE LIPS SINK SHIPS"?
WHAT THE HELL ARE YOU GOIN' ON ABOUT? THE BOY'S HARMLESS.

YORICK SAID HIS FRIEND WORKS FOR THE GOVERNMENT, LYDIA. SHE WAS PROBABLY SENT TO CHECK UP ON US.
AND IF OUTSIDERS FIND OUT WHO WE ARE... WHAT WE DID, WE'RE FUCKED.
SONIA SHOULD BE BACK WITH THEM ANY MINUTE. ONLY THING WE CAN DO NOW...

...IS MAKE SURE THEY NEVER LEARN THE TRUTH.

Boston, Massachusetts
Now

YEAH, BUT...NO.
HE'S NOT THE ENEMY, VICTORIA. YORICK'S MY--

UHF!

WHY... WHY DID YOU...?

DO YOU REMEMBER THE FIRST TIME YOU SAW HIS PENIS, HERO?

WAIT... WHAT?
THE LAST OF THE MEN. ASSUMING HE REALLY IS YOUR BLOOD RELATION, I IMAGINE YOU WERE EXPOSED TO HIS SEX ORGAN?
I... I'M NOT SURE. MAYBE. WHEN... WHEN I WAS JUST A--

DO YOU REMEMBER HOW YOU FELT WHEN HE SHOWED IT TO YOU, LOVE? YOU WERE DISGUSTED, WEREN'T YOU?
...YES?

YOU KNEW HE WAS A MONSTER THE MOMENT YOU SAW THAT HIDEOUS APPENDAGE.
IT WASN'T LIKE YOUR TEMPLE, HERO. HIS GROWTH USED THE SAME HOLE TO DISCHARGE WASTE AND SEED. AND WHY IS THAT?
BECAUSE SEMEN IS...IS POISON.

AND YOU DON'T WANT THIS CREATURE TO POISON ANY MORE OF YOUR SISTERS, DO YOU?
NO, I... I LOVE MY SISTERS.
THEN WHAT MUST THE DAUGHTERS OF THE AMAZON DO WITH THIS BROTHER OF YOURS?

KILL IT.
CYCLES
CHAPTER THREE
BRIAN K. VAUGHAN PIA GUERRA
WRITER/CO-CREATORS/PENCILLER
JOSE MARZAN JR., INKER
CLEM ROBINS, LETTERER PAMELA RAMBO, COLORIST
J.G. JONES, COVER ARTIST STEVE BUNCHE, EDITOR
Y: THE LAST MAN CREATED BY BRIAN K.VAUGHAN AND PIA GUERRA

Marrisville, Ohio
Eight Hours Later

YES.
I KNOW.

BUT SAVE YOUR GRATITUDE FOR *THESE* WOMEN.
THIS IS THE FIRST POST-PLAGUE MEDICAL FACILITY I'VE VISITED THAT DOESN'T LOOK LIKE IT BELONGS TO A FUCKING *MEDIEVAL BARBER*.
THAT'S ALL NINA, DR. MANN. MY GIRL KEEPS OUR WHOLE TOWN HEALTHY.

SONIA, WHY DON'T YOU GET SOME FIRE-WOOD FOR OUR VISITORS? FEELS LIKE THERE'S A COLD FRONT COMIN' IN.
SURE, LYDIA.
I CAN GIVE YOU A HAND. BE NICE TO TAKE A BREAK FROM MY PACING AND FRETTING...

SONIA, MAY I HAVE A WORD WITH YOU FIRST?
IN PRIVATE?

WHAT'S UP, TESS?
THE OUTSIDERS, YOU DIDN'T TELL THEM ANYTHING, DID YOU?

"OUTSIDERS"?
WHAT ARE YOU, PONY-BOY ALL OF A SUDDEN?
DID YOU TELL THEM ANY-THING?

NO. THE THREE OF US BARELY TALKED. WE WERE JUST WORRIED ABOUT GETTING THAT SECRET AGENT LADY BACK HERE.
WHY, WHAT ARE YOU FREAKING OUT ABOUT?

SONIA, WE DON'T KNOW ANYTHING ABOUT THIS GUY OR HIS... HIS "GOVERNMENT FRIENDS." THEY MAY HAVE COME HERE TO TAKE ALL OF THIS AWAY FROM US.
SO UNTIL WE CAN GET RID OF THEM...

...YOU KEEP YOUR MOUTH SHUT ABOUT WHO WE REALLY ARE.

EVERY-
THING OKAY BACK
THERE?
WITH TESS?
YEAH, SHE WAS JUST
REMINDING ME NOT TO
FART IN FRONT OF YOU
OR ANYTHING. BEEN A
WHILE SINCE
WE'VE HAD BOYS
AROUND.

HEY, HER AND THAT OTHER LADY, ARE THEY...?
PARTNERS? YEAH.
THAT A PROBLEM?

NO! NO, NOT AT ALL. I WAS JUST WONDERING, IS EVERYONE IN THIS TOWN, YOU KNOW...?
YORICK, IT WOULD TAKE A HELL OF A LOT MORE THAN ALL THE MEN DYING TO MAKE ME EAT PUSSY.
IS THAT WHAT YOU WERE TRYING TO ASK?

JEEZ, YOU, uh... DON'T BEAT AROUND THE BUSH, DO YOU?
SO TO SPEAK.

WHAT, DID YOU REALLY THINK I WAS SOME DAINTY LITTLE HOUSE ON THE PRAIRIE CHICK?
WELL, YOU ARE FROM MARRISVILLE, RIGHT?
ACTUALLY, THIS WAS SORT OF A...FORCED RELOCATION. I'M ORIGINALLY FROM CLEVELAND.

GET OUT! THAT'S WHERE I WAS BORN!
NO WAY.
SERIOUSLY! GO TRIBE, LET'S HANG OUT IN THE FLATS, ETC.?

SO...YOU'VE BEEN TO MARRISVILLE BEFORE?
NAH, I DIDN'T STAY IN OHIO THAT LONG. MY FAMILY'S PRETTY NOMADIC. BUT MY PARENTS MOVED BACK WHEN MY MOM RAN FOR CONGRESS.
I REMEMBER HER TALKING ABOUT THIS PLACE. YOU GUYS ARE FAMOUS FOR SOMETHING, RIGHT? LIKE YOUR PIEROGIES OR--

ACTUALLY, DO YOU MIND IF WE JUST GET TO WORK?

OH. YEAH. SURE, SONIA.
SORRY.

SORRY.

ARE YOU AWAKE?
I'M SO SORRY...

NO, I'M SORRY. IF I HADN'T HESITATED BEFORE JUMPING, YOU MIGHT NOT--
I'M SO SORRY...FOR ALL THE THINGS I'VE DONE.
IN EGYPT AND PANAMA AND...AND JORDAN.

YOU'RE DELIRIOUS, 355. YOU PROBABLY SHOULDN'T--
SHH.
I WANT YOU.

YOU... YOU DO?

I DON'T UNDERSTAND IT, BUT I *WANT* YOU...

I...I'M NOT SURE WHAT TO SAY.

I MEAN, OBVIOUSLY, YOU'RE A VERY--
I WANT YOU... YORICK.

YORICK?

UHN!

MAN, YOU SPLIT WOOD LIKE A GIRL.
FORGIVE ME, PAULA BUNYAN, BUT I'M AN ESCAPE ARTIST, NOT A FUCKING LUMBERJACK.

HEY, CAN YOU TEACH ME HOW TO ESCAPE?
FROM WHAT?

MARRISVILLE.

WHY WOULD YOU WANT TO LEAVE THIS PLACE? IT'S A GODDAMN *UTOPIA*.
YOU HAVEN'T SEEN US DURING OUR *PERIODS*. ALL OF OUR CYCLES ARE IN SYNCH, SO ONCE A MONTH, THIS TOWN TURNS INTO A BLOODY WHIRLPOOL OF BITCHINESS.

UM...
I'M *KIDDING*, YORICK. I LOVE IT HERE. THE ONLY REASON I WOULD EVER LEAVE IS TO BE WITH *YOU*.

OH.
WELL, I...I WISH YOU COULD, SONIA, BUT MY SITUATION IS KINDA... *COMPLICATED*.
YOU THINK I'D CRAMP YOUR STYLE, HUH?

WHAT DOES *THAT* MEAN?
IT'S COOL, YORICK. YOU'RE A GUY, MAYBE THE LAST ONE. IF I WERE YOU, I'D TRY TO BANG AS MANY GIRLS AS POSSIBLE, TOO. I WOULDN'T WANT JUST ONE CHICK WEIGHING ME DOWN.
NO, I TOLD YOU, I HAVE A--

A GIRLFRIEND, I KNOW BUT SHE'S OVERSEAS, AND YOU'RE HERE.
IT MUST BE... *HARD*.

YEAH.
IT...IT IS.

BUT FOR SOME RETARDED REASON, SOMEBODY UP THERE PICKED *ME* TO SURVIVE ALL THIS...SO I'M TRYING NOT TO TAKE ADVANTAGE OF THE SITUATION.
YOU BELIEVE IN *GOD?* AFTER EVERYTHING THAT *HAPPENED?*

I DON'T KNOW. I... I *USED* TO. I GUESS I'M ONE OF THOSE "RECOVERING CATHOLICS."
OH, SO ALL THIS "DEVOTION" TO YOUR GIRLFRIEND IS REALLY JUST SOME LEFTOVER HANG-UP ABOUT *SEX*.
MAYBE... BUT BETH WAS THE FIRST GIRL I EVER SLEPT WITH, YOU KNOW? SHE WAS THE ONLY WOMAN ALIVE WHO WANTED ME BACK WHEN I WAS JUST AN UNEMPLOYED LOSER. IF NOTHING ELSE, I THINK I OWE HER A LITTLE LOYALTY.

I'M SURE *LOTS* OF GIRLS WANTED YOU BACK THEN, YORICK.

THEY JUST DIDN'T KNOW HOW TO TELL YOU.

SO, ARE YOU GONNA DO A TRICK FOR ME, OR WHAT?
HOW? I DON'T HAVE HANDCUFFS OR A...A STRAIT-JACKET OR ANYTHING.
WHATEVER. JUST DO SOME-THING.

ALL RIGHT, I'LL BET YOU A HUNDRED DOLLARS I CAN GUESS WHAT COLOR UNDER-WEAR YOU HAVE ON.
YOU DON'T HAVE A HUNDRED DOLLARS.
FINE, I'LL BET YOU MY WATCH.

DEAL.
SO...WHAT ARE THEY?

LET'S SEE... YOUR PANTIES ARE... BLACK.

WRONG.
I'M NOT WEARING ANY PANTIES.

PROVE IT.

FORK OVER THE TIMEPIECE, KRESKIN.

ALL YOURS.

HEY.
THIS IS MY WATCH...

HOW DID YOU...?

I CAN'T DO THIS.
YOU...YOU CAN'T?

IT'S WRONG, YORICK.
YOU'RE ...YOU'RE RIGHT.
CHRIST, I'M SUCH AN ASSHOLE. I--

IT'S NOT *YOU*, YORICK. YOU'RE A...A REALLY GOOD PERSON.
TOO GOOD FOR SOMEONE LIKE *ME*.

WOW.
THERE'S A LINE I NEVER THOUGHT I'D HAVE TO HEAR AGAIN.

IT'S NOT LIKE THAT, YORICK. I'M A JUNKIE, OKAY? A...A FUCKING CRANK-HEAD.
I'M CLEAN NOW, BUT TRUTH IS, IF THERE WAS ANY WAY TO SCORE METH OUT HERE, I'D PROBABLY BE RIGHT BACK ON IT.

JESUS.
I...I'M SORRY. I HAD A COUSIN WHO DIED OF AN OVERDOSE.
THEN YOU'RE REALLY GONNA HATE ME, YORICK ...'CAUSE I'M ALSO A CONVICTED DEALER.

WHAT?

ME AND THIS GUY I WAS SEEING WERE BOTH USING. I HELPED COOK THE CRAP, BUT I ONLY EVER MADE ENOUGH FOR THE TWO OF US.
NOT THAT THAT'S AN EXCUSE. I...I KNOW IT WAS FUCKED UP. IT'S JUST...

MY BOYFRIEND STARTED SELLING ON THE SIDE WITHOUT TELLING ME, RIGHT? THE COPS EVEN-TUALLY PICKED HIM UP, AND IN EXCHANGE FOR A LESSER SENTENCE, HE TOLD THEM I WAS THE FUCKING RING-LEADER.
HE GOT FIFTEEN MONTHS... I GOT TEN YEARS.
SO WHAT ARE YOU SAYING? YOU'RE... YOU'RE SOME KIND OF ESCAPED CONVICT?

HAVEN'T YOU FIGURED IT OUT YET?
THAT'S WHAT EVERY WOMAN IN MARRISVILLE IS.

THIS IS A PRISON TOWN, YORICK. THERE'S A WOMEN'S FACILITY LESS THAN A MILE AWAY.
OH, FUCK...

WHEN ALL THE MEN DIED, THE WARDEN DECIDED TO TURN US LOOSE ...INSTEAD OF LETTING US STARVE TO DEATH IN OUR CELLS.
MOST OF THE GUARDS LIVED IN THE HOUSES WE'RE IN NOW. THEY TOOK OFF MONTHS AGO. I GUESS THEY COULDN'T STAND STAYING WHERE THEIR HUSBANDS AND... AND LITTLE BOYS DIED.

YORICK, NONE OF US WANTED TO GET OUT LIKE THIS... BUT IT HAPPENED.
THE OTHER INMATES AND I ALL GET ALONG PRETTY WELL, AND WE'VE BEEN TAKING CARE OF OURSELVES FOR YEARS, SO THIS COMMUNITY KINDA JUST FELL INTO PLACE.

I'M SORRY I DIDN'T TELL YOU SOONER, BUT YOU CAN UNDERSTAND WHY WE DON'T WANT PEOPLE TO KNOW. WE... WE JUST WANT TO GET ON WITH OUR LIVES.
SO PLEASE, YOU HAVE TO PROMISE TO KEEP THIS A SECRET, OKAY?

OKAY?

THEY'RE CRIMINALS!

WHAT THE HELL ARE YOU TALKING ABOUT, YORICK?
WHAT'S GOING ON HERE?
I'M SORRY, TESS. I...I THOUGHT I COULD TRUST HIM.

TELL HER.
I DON'T KNOW WHAT YOU'RE--
TELL HER WHAT YOU DID. OR I WILL.

...
ARMED ROBBERY.

WHAT?
HOW ABOUT YOU? WHAT WERE YOU IN FOR?
FRAUD. HEALTH CARE FRAUD. BUT I NEVER--

AND YOU?
WHAT DID YOU DO? KILL SOMEBODY?

YEAH. MY HUSBAND.
AND I DON'T REGRET IT FOR A GODDAMN SECOND.

YOU SEE, DOC! THESE WOMEN, THEY'RE ALL A BUNCH OF THIEVES AND...AND MURDERERS!
THEY STILL OWE A... A DEBT TO SOCIETY, DON'T THEY?

I MEAN, WHY THE HELL SHOULD THEY GET TO LIVE IN PARADISE?
THAT'S ENOUGH, YORICK.

YOU'RE COMING WITH ME... OR MY SISTERS AND I WILL SLAUGHTER EVERY WOMAN IN THIS TOWN.

Marrisville, Ohio
Now

UHN!

YORICK!

IT'S ALL RIGHT, SONIA. THIS IS MY SISTER.
SHE'S JUST... SHE'S JUST FUCKING AROUND.

I MEAN, THIS IS ALL SOME KIND OF JOKE, RIGHT?

IF IT IS...

32
...IT JUST GOT A LOT FUCKING FUNNIER.
UBV41
CYCLES
CHAPTER FOUR
BRIAN K. VAUGHAN PIA GUERRA
WRITER/CO-CREATORS/PENCILLER
JOSE MARZAN, JR., INKER
CLEM ROBINS, LETTERER PAMELA RAMBO, COLORIST
DIGITAL CHAMELEON, SEPARATOR
J.G. JONES, COVER ARTIST STEVE BUNCHE, EDITOR
Y: THE LAST MAN CREATED BY BRIAN K. VAUGHAN AND PIA GUERRA

I TOLD YOU, THE MALE COMES WITH ME OR MY SISTERS BURN THIS TOWN TO ASHES.

"THE MALE"?
WHAT THE FUCK IS WRONG WITH YOU, HERO?
I COULD ASK YOU THE SAME THING. I THOUGHT YOU WERE IN LOVE WITH BETH.

I AM! WHAT DOES THAT HAVE TO DO WITH--
I'VE BEEN TRAILING YOU FOR THE LAST HOUR, YORICK. I WATCHED YOU CHOP WOOD WITH THAT... THAT SONIA GIRL.
I SAW WHAT YOU DID TO HER.

IT WASN'T LIKE THAT! WE JUST--
RESIDENTS OF MARRISVILLE, A MOMENT OF YOUR TIME, PLEASE!

MY NAME IS VICTORIA. I ASSURE YOU, THE DAUGHTERS OF THE AMAZON AND I HAVE NO DESIRE TO HARM ANY WOMAN IN THIS TOWN.
AS A MATTER OF FACT, MY SISTERS AND I *ADMIRE* YOU!

AS OUR TRAIN WAS COMING INTO TOWN, WE PASSED A *WOMEN'S PENITENTIARY.* UNDOUBT-EDLY, ALL OF YOU ONCE RESIDED *INSIDE* OF IT.
FROM THE LOOKS OF YOUR COMMUNITY, YOU PEOPLE LONG AGO ESCAPED THE YOKE OF THE PATRIARCHY. NO DOTING WIFE OR BLUSHING BRIDE COULD HAVE BUILT THIS KINGDOM!

BELIEVE ME WHEN I TELL YOU THAT I *KNOW* HOW YOU SUFFERED AT THE HANDS OF MEN, JUST AS I KNOW HOW YOU *EVOLVED* ONCE FREE OF THEIR GRASP.
I KNOW THAT YOUR IMPRISONMENT WAS ALSO YOUR EMANCIPATION!
AND I KNOW THAT ONE OF OUR OPPRESSORS IS NOW IN YOUR MIDST.

YOUR ANIMAL INSTINCTS TELL YOU TO *PROTECT* THE BOY, BUT ASK YOURSELVES... ARE YOU ANIMALS OR ARE YOU *WOMEN?*
AFTER ALL, WHAT HAVE MEN EVER DONE FOR *YOU?*

FACT: THE VAST MAJORITY OF YOU CONVICTED OF VIOLENT CRIMES WERE MERELY DEFENDING YOURSELVES OR YOUR CHILDREN FROM AN ABUSIVE MALE.

FACT: THOSE OF YOU WHO KILLED YOUR HUSBANDS SERVED PRISON TERMS TWICE AS LONG AS MEN WHO KILLED THEIR WIVES.

FACT: MOST OF YOU WERE IN FOR "ECONOMIC CRIMES," LITERALLY STEALING TO FEED YOUR FAMILIES... BUT WHILE YOU ROTTED IN PRISON, MEN WHO EMBEZZLED BILLIONS WENT FREE.

FACT: IN THIS COUNTRY ALONE, MORE THAN 100,000 WOMEN WERE INCARCERATED BEFORE MOTHER EARTH CLEANSED HERSELF OF THE MALE ABOMINATIONS.

OVER THE LAST FEW MONTHS, HOW MANY GIRLS FORCED INTO DRUGS AND PROSTITUTION PERISHED, TRAPPED BEHIND BARS? AND FOR WHAT... MEN'S IDEA OF JUSTICE?

IF YOU WOMEN TRULY WANT TO REPAY YOUR "DEBT TO SOCIETY," YOU'LL HAND THE LAST OF THE MEN OVER TO ME.

BECAUSE ONCE YOU MAKE IT PAST THE SCALES AND THE BLINDFOLD... JUSTICE IS A WOMAN WITH A SWORD.

JESUS CHRIST.
WE'RE IN JOHN ASHCROFT'S HELL.

SO...WE DOING THIS HARD OR EASY?

HARD, ASSHOLE.
SONIA...

DID YOU HEAR ANYTHING VICTORIA JUST SAID?
EVERYTHING.
BUT JUST BECAUSE SOME STUCK-UP BITCH READS A FEW STATISTICS DOESN'T MEAN SHE KNOWS US.

SO UNLESS YOU'VE GOT ENOUGH ARROWS FOR EVERYONE IN THIS ROOM, YOU CAN GO OUT THERE AND TELL YOUR FRIENDS THAT WE'RE NOT GIVING UP ANY-ONE WITHOUT A FIGHT.

THAT...
THAT GOES FOR ALL OF YOU?

DAMN STRAIGHT.

THEN I'LL...I'LL LET VICTORIA KNOW.

I THINK SHE'S GONNA BE ANGRY.

WHAT THE FUCK IS *HAPPENING*...?

CAN WE SNEAK HIM OUT THE CELLAR EXIT?
UH-UH. PADLOCKED FROM THE OUTSIDE.
WAIT. WHAT ARE YOU TALKING ABOUT?

WHY?
SAVING YOUR ASS.
A...A FEW MINUTES AGO, I WAS SAYING THAT ALL OF YOU DESERVED TO BE LOCKED BACK UP.

YEAH, WELL, YOU'RE A SANCTIMONIOUS BRAT.
DON'T MEAN YOU DESERVE TO BE *EXECUTED*.

SO WHAT DO WE DO NOW?
RALLY THE TROOPS.
RIGHT. THERE ARE FOUR OF US FOR EVERY ONE OF THEM.

BUT THE BRA BURNERS OUT THERE HAVE WEAPONS.
DO...DO YOU?

NO ARMS IN MARRISVILLE.
IT WAS THE FIRST RULE IN OUR CHARTER.

YEAH, BUT AGENT 355--
--IS STILL UNCONSCIOUS, YORICK.
I KNOW, BUT SHE HAS A SHOTGUN AND SHIT IN HER--
--BACKPACK, WHICH I LEFT OUT BY THE TRACKS. I DIDN'T WANT TO WALK AROUND WITH A...A LOADED FIREARM.

I WAS AFRAID SOMEONE MIGHT GET HURT.

OKAY THEN.
I'M GOING OUT THERE.

BULLSHIT YOU ARE! THEY'LL MURDER YOU!
NOT NECESSARILY. HERO HAD A CHANCE TO KILL ME AND DIDN'T.
MAYBE I... MAYBE I CAN STILL TALK TO HER.

YORICK, YOUR SISTER, ALL OF THOSE GIRLS, THEY'RE STARVING AND BRAINWASHED AND--

WHAT AM I SUPPOSED TO DO, DOC? IF WE FIGHT, THEY'LL KILL US ALL, INCLUDING YOU.
BUT IF I GIVE MYSELF UP, YOU AND 355 CAN PRESS ON TO CALIFORNIA, MAYBE WORK YOUR CLONING MOJO WITHOUT ME.

WHATEVER HAPPENS...DON'T LET THOSE FUCKS TOUCH MY MONKEY.
NNN NNN

THIS ISN'T HIGH NOON, YORICK! YOU'RE BEING STUPID.
MAYBE, BUT THIS TOWN IS THE ONLY DECENT PLACE I'VE VISITED SINCE THE WORLD WENT TO SHIT. I DON'T WANT TO BE RESPONSIBLE FOR DESTROYING IT.
ANYWAY, I'M SORRY ABOUT THE THINGS I SAID BEFORE.
FOR A BUNCH OF FUCKING CRIMINALS, YOU LADIES ARE ALL RIGHT.
AND I'M SORRY ABOUT THE TWO TIMES I KISSED YOU, SONIA.
TWO TIMES? BUT YOU ONLY KISSED ME--

YOU SAID YOU WOULD HAVE "NO PROBLEM" GETTING YOUR SIBLING OUT HERE, HERO.
I KNOW, VICTORIA, BUT HE--

FORGET IT. WE'LL JUST TORCH THE ENTIRE GOD-DAMN HOSPICE AND--
RELAX, PSYCHO.

HERE COMES YOUR MAN.

DON'T YOU OPEN YOUR MOUTH TO HER!

GET ON YOUR KNEES!
I KNOW YOU'RE JUST ACTING, HERO. WHAT'S THE PLAN?

SHUT UP.
YOU WENT UNDERCOVER TO INFILTRATE THE AMAZONS, RIGHT? I FIGURED IT OUT, IT'S LIKE WHEN WE USED TO PLAY WITH YOUR BARBIES AND YOU'D PRETEND TO--

SHUT UP!
SWAK

...DAMMIT, HERO.

"ALAS, POOR YORICK..."

TELL ME YORICK, HAVE YOU EVER PLAYED CHESS?
AND WITH THAT, THE BATTLE OF THE SEXES ENTERS *ENDGAME*.
GEE, NEVER HEARD THAT ONE BEFORE ...YOU FUCKING *TWAT*.

YOU MADE HER WHAT SHE IS TODAY, RAPIST, NOT I.
YEAH, WITH MY SISTER, BEFORE YOU TURNED HER INTO A FUCKING *MONSTER*, YOU HATCHET-FACED PIECE OF *SHIT*!
AND NOW YOU WILL *PAY* FOR YOUR SINS, AND THE SINS OF *EVERY* MAN WHO EXPLOITED AND DEFILED OUR--

CHRIST ALMIGHTY!
YOU AMAZONS DON'T KNOW HOW TO SHUT UP AND KILL A GUY, DO YOU?

ON THE CONTRARY.
OBSERVE, SISTERS:

THE FALL OF MAN.

KLICK

THUNK

WHO...?

I... I DID IT.

SONIA.

YOU OKAY, KID?
YEAH, I--

AAAHHHH!

HERO, DON'T!

UHH

NO!

HEY!
ONE OF YOU MAKES ANOTHER MOVE, I KILL ALL YOU MOTHER-FUCKERS!
HOLD ON, SONIA. DR. MANN CAN--
IT'S ALL RIGHT, YORICK.
I...I BET YOUR GIRLFRIEND IS PRETTY.
I SAW THIS DOCUMENTARY ONCE. ON TV?
IT WAS ABOUT LIONS. THEY...THEY SAID THAT LIONS...

IS SHE...?

CAN I SEE THIS?
YORICK...

THANKS.

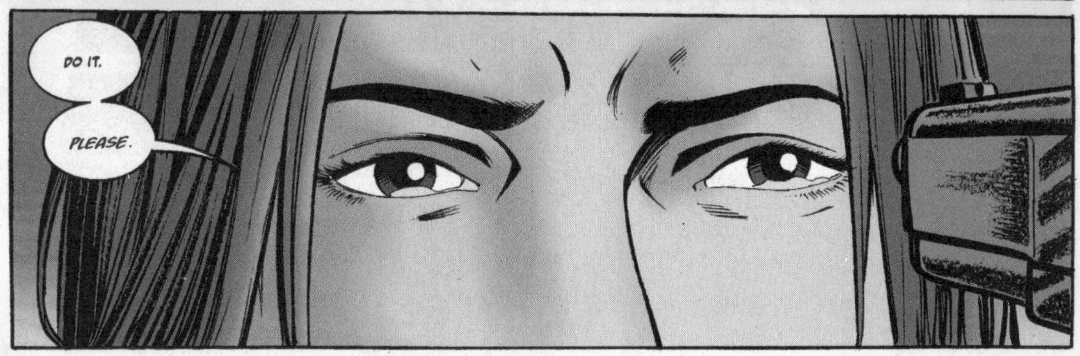
DO IT.
PLEASE.

P2K4 LOCKPICK

Marrisville, Ohio
Now

YORICK... PUT IT DOWN.

GET BACK INSIDE, DOC.

YORICK, SHE'S YOUR SISTER.
I DON'T CARE!

SHE SLAUGHTERED AN INNOCENT GIRL!

SIBLING OR NOT, SHE'S CROSSED THE FUCKING RUBICON.

THE WHAT?

SHUT UP, HERO.
I'M SERIOUS. WHAT IS THAT? "CROSSING THE RUBICON"?

IT'S JUST A SAYING, ALL RIGHT?
MEANS YOU'VE PASSED THE POINT OF NO RETURN...THAT YOU'RE *FUCKED.*
BUT *WHY* DOES IT MEAN THAT? WHAT'S A RUBICON?

JESUS CHRIST! YOU JUST *EXECUTED* ANOTHER HUMAN BEING, AND ALL YOU--

YOU DON'T KNOW...DO YOU?

DAD ALWAYS LIKED YOU BEST BECAUSE YOU WERE THE "SMART ONE"... BUT YOU'RE NOT THAT SMART.
YOU LOVE TO SHOW OFF ALL THE STUPID SHIT YOU MEMORIZE FROM BOOKS, BUT YOU DON'T REALLY *UNDERSTAND* THE WORLD. NOT LIKE I DO.

ME AND THE OTHER DAUGHTERS OF THE AMAZON, WE KNOW ABOUT *EVERYTHING* NOW...THANKS TO THE WOMAN YOUR LITTLE FUCK-BUDDY *KILLED*.

AND I KNOW THINGS EVEN *VICTORIA* DIDN'T KNOW. I KNOW ABOUT THE SACRED CAVE AND THE DANDELION LEAGUE AND THE... THE BACKWARDS EIGHT.
I KNOW WHY MOTHER EARTH DESTROYED *YOUR* KIND, AND I KNOW WHY *WE'RE* STILL HERE.

SO PULL THAT TRIGGER, YORICK. OTHERS WILL TAKE MY PLACE AFTER I'M GONE, AND ONE OF THEM *WILL* FINISH WHAT I STARTED WITH YOU.
MEN WILL BE EXTINCT SOON, BUT I'LL *NEVER* REALLY DIE.

YOU'RE WRONG, HERO.
KLICK

DAD ALWAYS LIKED *YOU* BEST.

BRIAN K. VAUGHAN PIA GUERRA
WRITER/CO-CREATORS/PENCILLER
JOSE MARZAN, JR., INKER

CLEM ROBINS, LETTERER **PAMELA RAMBO,** COLORIST
ZYLONOL, SEPARATOR
J.G. JONES, COVER ARTIST **STEVE BUNCHE,** EDITOR

Y: THE LAST MAN CREATED BY BRIAN K. VAUGHAN AND PIA GUERRA

WHAT... WHAT ARE YOU DOING?
YOU'RE SUPPOSED TO SHOOT ME.

HERE.
TAKE THIS.
AND DO WHAT WITH IT?

EVERYONE IN MARRISVILLE IS SOME SORT OF EX-CON, RIGHT? SONIA SAID YOUR OLD PENITENTIARY WAS CLOSE BY.
YEAH, BUT--
SO LOCK THESE PSYCHOS UP... AND THROW AWAY THE FUCKING KEY.

CAN'T DO IT, KID.

WHAT?
YOU HEARD ME. WHEN WE GOT SPRUNG AFTER THE PLAGUE, THIS TOWN VOWED NEVER TO DO WHAT HAD BEEN DONE TO US.
NEVER.

BUT THEY MURDERED SONIA!
HE'S RIGHT, LYDIA. THIS...THIS IS DIFFERENT. THEY'RE KILLERS.

SO AM I! AND I WANNA KILL AGAIN FOR WHAT THEY DID!
BUT LOOK AT THESE GIRLS. WITHOUT THE BITCH THAT'S BEEN CONTROLLING 'EM, THEY'RE NOTHING BUT FRIGHTENED. THEY NEED HELP, NOT A GODDAMN CELL.

WE'D BE HYPOCRITES TO PUT 'EM BEHIND BARS...AND SONIA WOULDA SAID THE SAME.
THAT'S INSANE! YOU CAN'T JUST--

WHAT-EVER.
DON'T BLAME ME WHEN THEY BURN THIS PLACE TO THE GROUND.

YORICK, WAIT!

YOU HAVE TO LISTEN TO HIM, LYDIA.
THESE PEOPLE ARE *ANIMALS*. BACK IN BOSTON, THEY BURNED DOWN MY ENTIRE *LABORATORY*.

THAT'S A LIE!
DON'T *EVEN*, ASS-HOLE.

HOLD ON, TESS.
LET HER TALK.

I WAS WITH THE AMAZONS EVERY STEP OF THE WAY IN BOSTON. WE DID A LOT OF THINGS... BUT WE NEVER TORCHED ANY LAB.
BULLSHIT.
YOU SAW ME KILL A GIRL. WHY WOULD I LIE ABOUT SOME *FIRE*?

WELL, IF YOU DIDN'T DO IT... WHO THE FUCK DID?

Massachusetts Air National Guard Base
Now

AIM FOR THE REAR ROTOR!
WHAT THE FUCK IS GOING ON?
MP

STAY DOWN!
BUNCH OF FOREIGNERS JUST STOLE A GODDAMN BLACK-HAWK!
WHAT? AL QAEDA'S HERE?

NO! THEY WERE TALKING JEWISH...uh, HEBREW!
ISRAELIS?
MP

THAT'S IMPOSSIBLE!
THEY'RE OUR ALLIES!

<LOOK, SADIE.>
<THEIR WOMEN HAVE EXCELLENT MARKSMANSHIP, BUT WATCH HOW THEY FLOUNDER IN THE ABSENCE OF LEADERSHIP... LIKE BEES WITHOUT A QUEEN.>
<LIEUTENANT-GENERAL TSE'ELON!>

<RADIO FOR YOU.>
<IT'S THE AMERICAN.>

JESUS, IS THAT GUNFIRE I HEAR? WHAT THE HELL ARE YOU DOING, ALTER? I TOLD YOU--
CALM YOURSELF, STRANGER. WE ARE KILLING NO ONE, ONLY LAYING DOWN SUPPRESSIVE FIRE FOR OUR ESCAPE.

ESCAPE? FROM WHAT?
YOU HAVE NOT EVEN REVEALED YOUR NAME TO ME. WHY SHOULD I TELL YOU ANYTHING?

BECAUSE IF YOU DON'T, I WON'T GIVE YOU THE CURRENT COORDINATES OF YORICK BROWN.

THE CRAFT THAT BROUGHT MY TROOPS TO THE STATES SUFFERED A BREAK-DOWN SO WE... *ACTIVELY ACQUIRED* AN ALTERNATE MEANS OF TRANSPORTATION.
NOW WHERE IS THIS MYTHICAL LAST MAN YOU PROMISED?

YOU KNOW HE'S NOT A MYTH, ALTER... OR YOU WOULDN'T STILL BE LOOKING FOR HIM.
NO, I WOULD BE LOOKING FOR **YOU**, AND I PROMISE THAT YOU WOULD NOT BE PLEASED TO SEE ME.
RELAX, SOLDIER. WE'RE ALL ON THE SAME SIDE HERE.

THE BOY IS IN A SMALL TOWN IN NORTHERN OHIO CALLED MARRISVILLE.
YOU'RE POSITIVE? WHERE DOES YOUR INTELLIGENCE COME FROM?
I CAN'T TELL YOU THAT, BUT I **CAN** TELL YOU THAT YOU'LL HAVE TO MOVE QUICKLY.
I DON'T THINK HE'LL BE THERE LONG...

THE RUBICON.

IT'S A RIVER IN ITALY.

355.
CAESAR CROSSED IT TO CONFRONT HIS OLD FRIEND POMPEY, PLUNGED THE ROMAN REPUBLIC INTO CIVIL WAR.

YOU SAW WHAT HAPPENED ?
DR. MANN TOLD ME.
I ONLY REGAINED CONSCIOUSNESS A LITTLE WHILE AGO.

ARE YOU...?
STILL DIZZY, BUT I SHOULD BE 100% AGAIN BEFORE LONG.

YORICK, I... I'M SO SORRY I WASN'T THERE FOR YOU. I'LL NEVER FORGIVE MY-SELF FOR--

FORGET IT, JAKE.
IT'S MARRISVILLE.

"JAKE"?
HOW CAN SOMEONE KNOW RUBICON BUT NOT CHINATOWN?

WHAT'S WITH THE SCISSORS?
HUH? OH. I FOUND 'EM IN SONIA'S ROOM AND I THOUGHT... WHATEVER. IT'S STUPID.
I HAVEN'T GOTTEN MY HAIR CUT SINCE ALL THE BARBERS DIED, AND FOR SOME REASON I SUDDENLY FELT LIKE--

HERE. LET ME.
YOU HAVE TIME TO PLAY *STYLIST*? SHOULDN'T YOU BE BACK IN TOWN, MAKING SURE THE ROAD WARRIORS DON'T START RAPING AND PILLAGING?
THE LOCALS ALREADY INCARCERATED THEM, YORICK.

SERIOUSLY?
APPARENTLY, EVERYONE REACHED A COMPROMISE. THEY'RE GOING TO DETAIN ALL THE AMAZONS FOR THE TIME BEING, AND STAGGER RELEASES AS INDIVIDUALS ARE DEEMED READY TO BE REINTRODUCED TO SOCIETY.

AND YOU'RE *OKAY* WITH THAT? I THOUGHT YOU WERE SUPPOSED TO BE MS. LAW & ORDER!
YORICK, THIS COUNTRY'S PRISON SYSTEM WAS AN EMBARRASSMENT. I'D CONSIDER JUST ABOUT ANY ALTERNATIVE MORE REASONABLE.
HOW CAN YOU *SAY* THAT? A FEW HOURS AGO, I WAS STANDING HERE TALKING WITH A GIRL, AND NOW SHE'S FUCKING *GONE*! ALL BECAUSE ONE OF THOSE *SAVAGES*...

ALL BECAUSE OF MY SISTER.

I ACTUALLY CAUGHT A GLIMPSE OF HERO BEFORE THEY PUT HER AWAY.
SHE HAD THIS... THIS *LOOK* ON HER FACE THAT REMINDED ME OF SOME-THING I SAW ONCE, DURING MY FIRST ASSIGNMENT FOR THE CULPER RING. I WAS JUST A KID.

IT WAS IN WACO BACK IN '93, RIGHT BEFORE THE FBI'S FUCK-UP. I HAD TO INFILTRATE THE COMPOUND AND EXTRACT A SENATOR'S NIECE WHO HAD FALLEN IN WITH KORESH.
THE RING GAVE ME PLENTY OF PHOTOS OF THE GIRL...BUT WHEN I FINALLY FOUND HER, SHE LOOKED *NOTHING* LIKE THE PICTURES.

HER EYES WERE DEAD, YORICK. SHE CLEARLY WASN'T THE PERSON SHE USED TO BE. BUT AFTER A FEW MONTHS OF DEPROGRAMMING--
I APPRECIATE WHAT YOU'RE TRYING TO DO, 355, BUT IT DOESN'T CHANGE MY MIND.
I MEAN, I'M AS LIBERAL AS THE NEXT NADERITE...BUT *FUCK* THAT PATTY HEARST SHIT. MY SISTER IS RESPONSIBLE FOR WHAT SHE DID. SHE DESERVES TO BE PUNISHED.

THEN WHY DIDN'T YOU SHOOT HER?
BECAUSE MY MOTHER--*OUR* MOTHER --TAUGHT HERO AND ME THAT NO ONE SHOULD DIE FOR THEIR CRIMES.

BETTER TO LET THEM ROT IN PRISON FOR THE REST OF THEIR MISERABLE LIVES.

HHH...
AHUH...

HWUHHH
HERO, ARE ...ARE YOU PUKING?

MY... MY BROTHER...
I KNOW. WE'LL FIND A WAY TO GET HIM, HERO. AS SOON AS THEY LET US OUT OF HERE, WE'LL--
YOU DON'T UNDERSTAND. MY BROTHER... IS AN ESCAPE ARTIST.

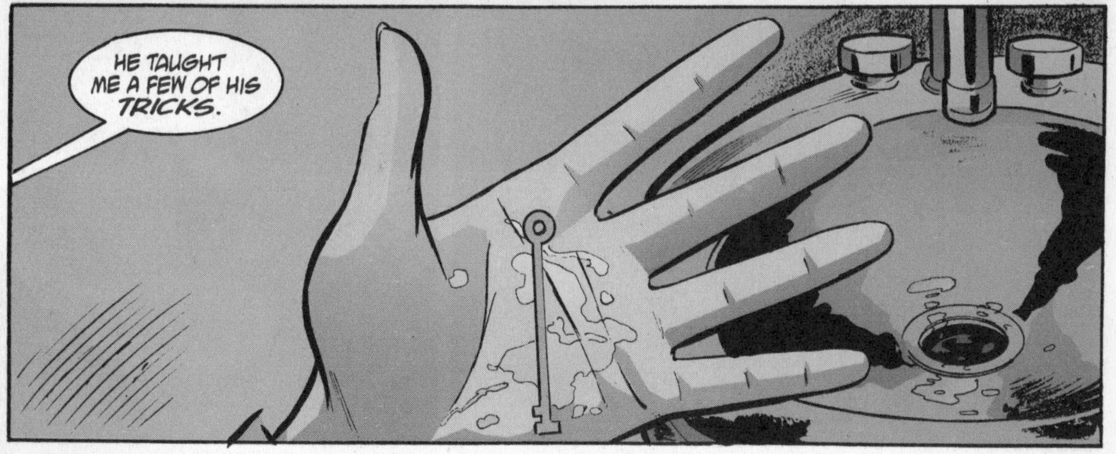
HE TAUGHT ME A FEW OF HIS TRICKS.

BUT WE REALLY HAVE TO LEAVE *TONIGHT?* I MEAN, YOU'RE STILL RECOVERING AND--
THE TOWNSPEOPLE TRADED A LOT OF PRODUCE TO GET US ON THE NEXT TRAIN TO CALIFORNIA. WE CAN'T AFFORD TO TURN THEM DOWN.

I KNOW. IT'S JUST, I WAS SORTA HOPING WE COULD STICK AROUND FOR SONIA'S FUNERAL.
I'M SORRY, YORICK, BUT THE ONLY THING THAT SPREADS FASTER THAN THE PLAGUE IS RUMORS ABOUT *LIVING MEN.*
WE HAVE TO GET OUT OF HERE BEFORE THE CURIOUS HORDES COME LOOKING FOR YOU.

'EVENING. AFRAID THE OTHERS ARE STILL DOWN AT THE PRISON, BUT I WAS ABLE TO GET YOU THE ENTIRE CABOOSE TO YOURSELVES.
DR. MANN AND YOUR ANIMAL ARE ALREADY INSIDE.
THANK YOU, MA'AM. AS SOON AS THE GOVERNMENT IS UP AND RUNNING AGAIN, I'LL SEE THAT YOUR TOWN IS REPAID FOR ITS KINDNESS.

YOU'LL FORGIVE ME IF I DON'T HOLD MY BREATH.
YEB VAS! GET YOUR HANDS OFF OF ME!

WHAT'S GOING ON?
OH, THE BULLS HAVE STARTED CHECKING THE BOXCARS FOR FREELOADERS BEFORE PULLING OUT. IT'S NOTHING.

NO! PLEASE!
I COME ALL THE WAY FROM MOSCOW! I NEED TO GET TO THE KANSAS! THE SOYUZ IS COMING TO--
JUST GET OFF THE TRAIN, LADY!

ANYWAY, YOU BETTER SETTLE IN BEFORE THE ALL-ABOARD, YORICK.
I JUST WANTED TO SAY, NINA, IF YOU'RE LOOKING FOR SOMETHING TO PLAY AT, YOU KNOW, AT SONIA'S WAKE, BOWIE WOULD BE GOOD.
SHE... SHE LIKED DAVID BOWIE.

AND PLEASE TELL EVERYONE HOW SORRY I AM FOR...FOR THE SUFFERING I BROUGHT.
IT'S ALL RIGHT, YORICK.

JUST TRY NOT TO TAKE TOO MUCH OF IT WITH YOU.

CAN'T SLEEP THROUGH 355'S SNORING EITHER, HUH?
NAH, JUST THINKING ABOUT MY GIRLFRIEND.

THE ONE IN THE OUTBACK?
YEAH. I KNOW YOU PROBABLY THINK I'M A SHITTY BOYFRIEND AFTER EVERYTHING THAT'S HAPPENED...BUT BETH REALLY IS THE ONLY PERSON IN THE WORLD FOR ME.
I'M SURE OF THAT NOW. WHENEVER I LOOK UP AT THE STARS, I WONDER IF SHE'S OUT THERE, LOOKING UP AT THE SAME ONES.

WELL, CONSIDERING IT'S THE MIDDLE OF THE *AFTERNOON* IN AUSTRALIA, I'D SAY THAT'S PRETTY UNLIKELY, DON JUAN.

YOU KNOW, FOR HALF A SECOND, I WAS STUPID ENOUGH TO THINK THIS LAST BOY ON EARTH GIG MIGHT BE *FUN*...

220 Miles above Earth
Now

THAT'S IT. THE ELEKTRON'S GONE FROM WORKING INTERMITTENTLY TO BELCHING *HYDROGEN* INTO THE CABIN, AND WE'RE DOWN TO ONLY HALF A S.F.O.G. CARTRIDGE.
EVEN THE GODDAMN HAM RADIO'S DEAD.
WELL THEN, THE CHOICE HAS BEEN MADE FOR US...

...WE'RE GOING BACK TO EARTH.

: THE SKETCHBOOK

Preliminary character designs and sketches from co-creator and penciller **Pia Guerra.**

Yorick and Ampersand
PAGUERRA
Early Yorick

EARLY
BETH
AND YORICK

PAGUERRA
First design
for 355

early
Revised 355
Pia Guerra
355
developing
Pia Guerra

FIRST SKETCH
DR. MANN
PIA GUERRA

THE REPORTER
ALTER
SADIE
FROZAN HAMAD
HERC' PILOT

"HELENE"
ORIGINAL SCRIPT HAD THE AMULET BEING A SMALL STATUE WITH AFGHAN/MINOAN/PERSIAN INFLUENCES.
MINOAN/PERSIAN CROSS

Amazons
PIA GUERRA